BRITAIN'S HERITAGE

Narrow Gauge Locomotives

Anthony Coulls

AMBERLEY

Acknowledgements

The author would like to thank Gareth Jones, fellow Talyllyn engineman, for the cover image of Talyllyn Railway No. 7 *Tom Rolt* climbing Brynglas Bank on 1 September 2017. Thanks also to the Vale of Rheidol Railway Archive and Robert Bance for the image of the Ruston Proctor locomotive. All other photographs were taken by the author or Peter Coulls, or are from the Peter Coulls collection. I would also like to thank Peter Coulls for proof reading and general assistance, and Nick Wright for his patience during the production of this book when a trip to Istanbul intervened.

This book is dedicated to all the friends I have made on the narrow gauge railways across the country over the last thirty years, and my parents, Peter and Janet, who encouraged and supported that interest when I made it a practical interest by joining the Locomotive Department of the Talyllyn Railway.

First published 2018

Amberley Publishing
The Hill, Stroud
Gloucestershire, GL5 4EP

www.amberley-books.com

Copyright © Anthony Coulls, 2018

The right of Anthony Coulls to be identified as the Author of this work has been asserted in accordance with the Copyrights, Designs and Patents Act 1988.

ISBN 978 1 4456 7556 5 (paperback)
ISBN 978 1 4456 7557 2 (ebook)

British Library Cataloguing in Publication Data.
A catalogue record for this book is available from the British Library.

Printed in the UK.

Contents

1
Introduction: Origins of the Narrow Gauge

Narrow gauge railways have long been a source of fascination for many. From famous public lines such as the Ffestiniog Railway and Lynton & Barnstaple Railway, to peat extraction lines in Cumbria and brickworks systems on Humberside, the narrow gauge railway has transcended two centuries. Ubiquitous in its day, but so often unseen, the attraction is unique. Narrow gauge is defined as anything less than the standard gauge of UK main lines – usually down to 15 inch gauge – but in that spectrum there is no limit to size, simplicity or shape. These were machines built to do a job, pure and simple, but those jobs were many and varied. Multiple wheeled complex engines could share a track with a simple motorised wagon, while all manner of propulsion could be found – steam, diesel, petrol and electric – even fireless, compressed air or steam locos converted to electric power. This book looks at them and their legacy today across the plethora of pleasure and heritage lines that exist.

In the beginning, there was no standard gauge, broad gauge or narrow gauge. Narrow gauge lines existed right from the earliest days of the railway in the UK, going back to 1604,

Other than manpower, the original narrow gauge form of propulsion was the horse. Here's Truman, recreating the days of the Corris, Machynlleth & River Dyfi Tramroad for the 150th anniversary of the opening of that line, which became the Corris Railway.

and could be found in mines, collieries and quaysides but were not known as such. It was only after the adoption of 4 feet 8½ inches as the 'standard' gauge, or 'Stephenson' gauge, in the 1820s that anything other than that gained the terms described. Narrow gauge is a very broad church indeed – and in practical terms of locomotives can go down as far as 15 inches, usually the domain of pleasure and miniature lines. Therefore this book will be guided by purpose rather than gauge as some minimum gauge locomotives existed which were considered the smallest practical for serious commercial work. The first 'narrow gauge' steam locomotive was not realised as such, as there was no 'standard' in 1803, but it wasn't long before the wider option so common in the North East became prevalent. The steam locomotive in general was developed to suit that standard.

As the railway developed into a common carrier in the 1830s, the standard gauge influence grew and narrow gauge as we know it today emerged in 1836. That year a slate-carrying railway in Wales opened to run 13 miles from the quarries to a port on the coast – what became the world-famous Ffestiniog Railway. A narrow gauge line could be built much more economically than a wider gauge, and with tighter curves and steeper gradients. Initially operated by horse power and gravity, it was not thought practical to use steam at first. In 1863, after consideration and competition, a small steam locomotive appeared; built by George England in London, it had a long journey to North Wales, but soon proved its worth.

In the museum of the Welsh Highland Heritage Railway at Porthmadog, a Ffestiniog Railway dandy car and slate wagon remind us of the origins of the latter railway, opened in 1836 and horse-powered for nearly three decades.

151 years of narrow gauge locomotive heritage in one photograph! At the 2017 Shrewsbury Steam Rally, a working replica of the 1803 Coalbrookdale Trevithick locomotive from the Ironbridge Museums Trust ran alongside a 1954 Hunslet 2-6-2 tank engine, new to the Sierra Leone Railways and now owned by the Welshpool & Llanfair Railway. Despite its colonial heritage, the design went back nearly fifty years and mirrored Hunslet's production for the home market.

Did you know?

On the Ffestiniog Railway, the horse pulled the empty trains of wagons uphill from the port to the quarries in Blaenau Ffestiniog. Mercifully for the horse, the laden trains travelling downhill by gravity had a special wagon, called a dandy, for the horse to ride in at the back of the train.

2

The Fascination of Steam

Though the railway, in the sense of a prepared way which guides and supports wheeled vehicles, can be traced back to classical antiquity, and is attested in the United Kingdom from 1604, it was only with the evolution of the steam railway locomotive that it began to emerge as the dominant transport medium in the developed world. The steam railway locomotive owes its origin to the Cornish engineer Richard Trevithick, who developed the stationary steam plant devised by Thomas Newcomen and James Watt in such a way as to make high pressure steam, and practical self-propelling units, a reality. The first successful rail-based steam locomotive was Trevithick's Coalbrookdale engine of 1803, still disputed as having existed by many, and by later standards, it could be judged as narrow gauge too – being 3 feet between the plate rails it ran upon. A working replica now exists at Blists Hill Open Air Museum in Ironbridge. This was the forerunner to the much better-known Pen y Darren locomotive of 1804. Contemporary drawings of the Coalbrookdale engine are quite clear about the gauge, which was the track gauge of many of the Shropshire tramways and rail ways. Initially only to be found on short-haul colliery railways, by the late 1820s locomotives had advanced sufficiently to be the motive power of choice on the new inter-urban systems, and other than in industrial applications, these were standard gauge or more. It was the ground-breaking Ffestiniog Railway that introduced steam on common-carrying public narrow gauge railways in 1863, followed by the Talyllyn Railway in 1864.

By the mid-1860s a variety of locomotive types were available, including tank locomotives purpose-designed for industrial service, such as in mine-yards, quarries and factories, for gauges of between 1 foot 6 in. and 7 feet. Very often these designs were sufficiently good as to require very little adaptation for the best part of a century.

From the early years of the twentieth century, steam locomotives were increasingly challenged by new forms of motive power, in particular electric and internal combustion units.

The two major players in the narrow gauge steam pioneers were the Ffestiniog Railway and Talyllyn Railway. Locomotives from the two railways have rarely met, and until 2015, never on home ground! Here are *Palmerston* and *Dolgoch* side by side at the standard gauge Llangollen Railway, where the two were running together for a gala in 2012.

The steam locomotive was numerically dominant on the railways of the developed world as late as 1950, but within ten years had either disappeared or was in sharp retreat. British Railways effectively finally dispensed with steam in 1968, though the last steam locomotives in industrial service in the UK were still at work in the 1980s. Steam locomotives are now only to be found in revenue-earning main line service in a few countries of the world, such as China, Burma and Poland, and in industrial service in a dwindling number of locations, mainly in the developing world. Many of these were of narrow gauge, some Chinese steam locomotives being constructed into the 1990s. In the UK, narrow gauge steam in commercial use, other than on tourist railways, only just outlasted main line steam, with the last industrial systems of Bowaters Paper, Dinorwic Quarry and BICC ceasing operation at the end of the 1960s.

The initial use of narrow gauge steam in the form of the George England tank and tender locomotives on the Ffestiniog Railway in 1863 ensured that the take-off of commercial narrow gauge steam was rapid on an international scale. In the beginning, the use of steam on anything other than standard gauge on a statutory railway was unusual, if not unheard of. The growing traffic on the Ffestiniog saw the need for relief of the horses used as motive power. The London company of George England provided a pair of small 0-4-0 type tank locomotives with separate coal tenders, which were shipped to Wales and then brought by horse and cart to Porthmadog for trial and entrance into traffic – *The Prince* and *The Princess* carved themselves a place in history and both still survive into the twenty-first century, albeit after much modification and adaptation over a long working life. *The Prince*, its name now shortened simply to *Prince*, is one of the oldest working steam locomotives in the world and the oldest in the UK. In the following year, 1864 saw the delivery of Fletcher Jennings saddle tank loco *Talyllyn* for use on the first narrow gauge railway designed for steam locomotion from the outset. Four wheels on occasion became six, side and saddle tanks abounded, with carrying trucks under cabs and fireboxes, and the scene was set for continued development – of both public narrow gauge railways and industrial systems large and small – sometimes with the two overlapping significantly.

Two locomotives for the price of one was what was really needed on tight curves and sharp gradients and it was once more the George England company that came up with the goods to the design of Robert Fairlie. An articulated locomotive – an engine that could bend to traverse tight curves – was the result and a plethora of similar and different designs grew, and the first Fairlie, *Little Wonder*, ran on the Ffestiniog Railway in 1869. A series of trials were

Talyllyn Railway locomotive No. 1 *Talyllyn* was built in 1864, just a year after the Ffestiniog introduced narrow gauge steam. Here it is at Tywyn Wharf station between the wars.

Double Fairlie twin-ended locomotives are synonymous with the Ffestiniog Railway. Not long into the preservation era, *Earl of Merioneth* was put back into working order and was seen at Portmadoc station in 1958 by the late Tom Charman.

run between the conventional four wheeled tank engines and the eight wheeled Fairlie. C. E. Spooner chronicled the results in his book *Narrow Gauge Railways*, published in 1871. The trials were attended by railway engineers from across the globe with the result that Fairlies went worldwide, but if you want to see one in action in the twenty-first century, you have to go back to where it all began – the Ffestiniog Railway. It still operates *Merddin Emrys*, built in the railway's own workshop in 1879, plus two others built in the twentieth and twenty-first century, proving the durability of the design and its suitability for purpose. There are two types – the double Fairlie with the back-to-back arrangement and look, then the more conventional single Fairlie, which looks like a normal tank locomotive to all intents and purposes until one begins to look at its construction and engineering. The Fairlie saw mainly passenger use, being less suited to goods and industrial traffic, being a bit of a refined creature.

Did you know?

The Ffestiniog Double Fairlie locomotives carry their names in English on one side and Welsh on the other.

At the other end of the scale, the narrow gauge locomotive began to lend itself to industrial purposes away from the public common-carrying railways. Small four and six wheeled tank engines began to be made by Hunslet, Manning Wardle, Peckett and many other manufacturers. Taking the place of men or horses, a tank locomotive and wagons could – and did – move anything, from slate to night soil.

Above: The small industrial tank engine is epitomised by the Quarry Hunslet type. Simple and rugged, they lasted a long time in service, many surviving into the heritage period. Here are two examples, *Edward Sholto* and *Hugh Napier*, together at Beamish Museum in April 2015.

Left: Down in Dorset, a number of lines served the ball clay industry, with some incredible locomotives. This is *Secundus*, built by Bellis & Seekings of Birmingham and now preserved in the museum at Corfe Castle.

On the clay railways, engines from another era worked on into the 1950s on many occasions. Here's a locally built Lewin of Poole 0-4-0 pulling full wagons of clay.

Did you know?

Manchester Corporation had an entire narrow gauge railway system which took night soil from the city out to Chat Moss, where it was dumped.

While tank locomotives prevailed, side, saddle and well tanks all finding use, the oddities also found favour with some customers. Vertical boilers were utilised when an engineering firm used to making cranes or winches adapted existing products, as the marine engineers De Winton of Caernarfon did. Tens of their locomotives were built, mostly working in the local slate and granite industries, but finding their way as far as Derbyshire and Scotland on later applications. Long life saw some of these simple but hardy locomotives work through eight decades, eventually finding their way into preservation in the 1960s. One still remains, stranded in the granite quarries high above Penmaenmawr in North Wales, inaccessible to all but the most determined. Thrift also saw a number of Foden and Sentinel steam lorries converted to rail use.

The small tank engine of 2 or 3 foot gauge with four-wheel side tipper trucks or, latterly, vee-shaped skip wagons became the vehicle of industry, wherever there were large civil engineering projects, dams, reservoirs, railways, airfields. Brickyards and gasworks, the narrow gauge steam locomotive knew them all, and manufacturers began to develop standard ranges of designs, for a variety of gauges and applications. Thus it was that Bagnalls of Stafford, for example, created a type of four wheeled saddle tank locomotive that was as much at home in an Indian colliery as it was in a Warwickshire sewage works. Avonside and

The De Winton make from Caernarfon owed much of its origins to marine practice, and vertical boilered engines became the norm for them. The remains of their locomotive *Llanfair* were seen in May 2010 at Dinas on the Welsh Highland Railway.

Bagnall saddle tank locos were one of the standard types found throughout industry and across the world. *Woto* worked in Kent throughout its commercial career and is now owned by Patrick Keef, who takes it to heritage railways to run on occasion. May 2016 saw it working a short demonstration goods train at Threlkeld Quarry museum in Cumbria.

Barclay built similar light four wheeled tank engines up until the 1930s, and even after their original purposes might have ended, the second-hand market for narrow gauge locomotives was fairly prosperous, either through sales from the works after reconditioning or through dealers such as J. F. Wake of Darlington and Dunns of Bishop Auckland, who sold steam locomotives from Durham County Council reservoir projects to the slate quarries of North Wales. Likewise, Kerr Stuart 'Wren' types found use from brickworks and smelters to a small fleet operated by Devon County Council on road improvement schemes. Similarly, a large number of contracting locomotives were run by the construction giant McAlpines and throughout the 1920s and 1930s, steam and internal combustion locomotives could be found on civil engineering and road building projects, including the Guildford bypass.

The smallest locos were of below 2 foot gauge and the gauges of 15 inches and 18 inches found favour – the former through the work of Sir Arthur Heywood and the latter from a

The Kerr Stuart 'Wren' design was another light locomotive that saw extensive use on temporary contractor's lines as well as established industrial systems. Beamish Museum's April 2010 display consisted of two Wrens, working on a portable line constructed for a steam event. The grey engine worked in Derbyshire and is now part of the Vale of Rheidol Railway collection, whereas the green engine, *Peter Pan*, was in the service of Devon County Council for quarrying and roads construction and is now owned by Graham Morris.

number of other commercial builders. Heywood was an exponent of the minimum gauge railway and he believed that 15 inches was the smallest size a line could be built to and be commercially viable. Only a couple of lines were built with his equipment, but enough to make a significant contribution to narrow gauge history. 18 inch gauge was used in a number of applications, perhaps the best known being the Deptford Meat Depot, whose locos were then sold to the Sand Hutton Railway in Yorkshire, and the similar Hunslet well tank locos in use at John Knowles' works in Derbyshire. The railway works lines at Crewe and also Horwich were the same gauge, as was the internal factory railway of locomotive manufacturing giant Beyer Peacock.

Stephen Lewin of Poole built some very unconventional locomotives with single cylinders mounted on top of their boilers, rather akin to traction engine practice, although oddly enough they never made a traction engine! They also built twin cylinder locomotives with cylinders in the conventional position under the boiler. Two replicas of these, *Ant* and *Bee*, run on the Laxey Mines Railway on the Isle of Man, very small machines for limited clearances and headroom. By contrast, some of the existing manufacturers of traction engines, such as Aveling & Porter, also made locomotives based on their standard road-going machines.

Did you know?

After the high profile Ffestiniog Railway, one of the first innovative uses of narrow gauge railways was at the Crewe Works of the London & North Western Railway. Small 18 inch gauge 0-4-0 tank locomotives were made in the 1860s by the works for use in transporting materials and components around the works. Crewe North signal box was bisected by a bridge for the works railway, known locally as the 'Midge Bridge' as Midge was the name of one of the small locomotives.

Above: Taking narrow gauge to another level, the 18-inch gauge was successfully used commercially in a number of applications. The clay works of John Knowles at Woodville in Derbyshire ran this Hunslet loco, *Jack*, on their system until the 1950s. It returned to the city of its manufacture for preservation at Armley Mills Museum, where it was steamed by the author for test in March 2015.

Below: At the National Railway Museum in York, one of the 18-inch gauge works locomotives from Horwich in Lancashire greets visitors at the main entrance. A picture of it at work can be seen on the adjacent wall.

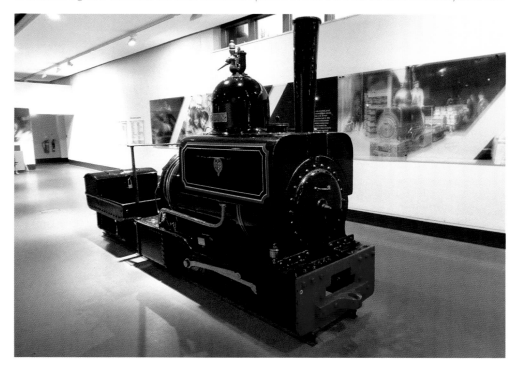

Although no Stephen Lewin of Poole narrow gauge locomotves still exist, Beamish Museum and Dave Young built a full size working replica of one that worked in Weardale. Completed in 2016, it visited the Ffestiniog Railway in May 2017.

Away from industry, the narrow gauge railway began to find favour with public lines carrying both goods and passengers in areas where it was indeed uneconomic to build a standard gauge line. Wales, hilly parts of England and other outlying areas all saw narrow gauge lines created, mostly up to around 20 miles in length. The Southwold, Leek & Manifold and Lynton & Barnstaple are amongst the best known, along with the Vale of Rheidol Railway, the Welshpool & Llanfair Light Railway and the Campbeltown and Machrihanish line in Scotland. All of these had locomotives befitting of their status, being far from pottering small tank engines. UK narrow gauge tender locomotives were very unusual. Tank engines were the main permutation found, like the Manning Wardle-made engines on the short-lived Ffestiniog & Blaenau Railway. The final 2-6-2 Vale of Rheidol machines weighed more than 25 tons apiece, and shared common components with the Great Western Railway's standard gauge steam railmotor units. Still only on the nominal 2 foot gauge, the Lynton and Barnstaple 2-6-2 tanks were similarly sized, as was the one-off *Russell* of the Porthmadog, Beddgelert & South Snowdon Railway – a very handsome machine, which influenced the 2-6-2 tank engines made by Hunslet for export to Sierra Leone.

Some of the larger industrial concerns had big locos too, Harrogate Gasworks operating an 0-6-2 saddle tank by Greens of Leeds, and the various clay lines of Purbeck running quite large machines. Kettering Furnaces in Northamptonshire had a fleet of 3 foot gauge saddle tanks and the general East Midlands ironstone industry saw a large number of similar lines, some running for a number of miles with larger tank engines from such

Above: The Kitson of Leeds-built Leek & Manifold Railway locomotives had their origins in the colonial designs of E. R. Calthrop, clearly seen in the massive headlamp and style of the loco cab amongst other things. Far from a quaint undertaking, these were massive engines, with similar machines operating in India.
Below: On the Isle of Man, the classic lines of the Beyer Peacock 2-4-0 tank engine have been seen in operation since the railways opened there in the 1870s. Still in operation today, there are many people for whom this is the ultimate classic narrow gauge locomotive.

Above: In narrow gauge lore, the Lynton & Barnstaple Railway in North Devon is a legend, having closed in the 1930s and all its locomotives having been scrapped. The 2-6-2 tank loco *Taw* was equally at home running in either direction. Built by Manning Wardle in Leeds, it was similar to a number of UK common carrier railway locos on the narrow gauge.

Below: The Vale of Rheidol Railway runs from Aberystwyth on the Welsh coast and is very similar to several narrow gauge lines built at the end of the nineteenth century. Their original locomotives were made by Davies & Metcalfe and were very like the Lynton & Barnstaple engines. Replaced in the 1920s by Great Western Railway-built machines, original loco No. 1212 is seen at Swindon works at the end of its life.

A variant on the 2-6-2 theme is *Russell*, built for the Porthmadog, Beddgelert & South Snowdon Railway in 1906. It latterly worked for the Welsh Highland Railway and worked its way into preservation via the Hook Norton ironstone mines and the Purbeck clay industry. Finally restored to full glory, it visited the Talyllyn Railway for their 150th anniversary celebrations and is seen there in July 2015.

Not all industrial locomotives were small tank engines. Harrogate Gas Works ran this large 0-6-2 made by Greens of Leeds, better known for their lawnmowers, road rollers and steam trams! It's now at the South Tynedale Railway, where it was seen in May 2012, part way through restoration which has now been completed.

makers as Peckett, Hudswell Clarke and Bagnall. There were even a couple of imports from French tramways that made an appearance on the Eastwell ironstone system. The Snailbeach District Railways in Shropshire also were an important player on the scene and survived long enough to purchase army surplus steam locomotives, which largely supplanted their Kerr Stuart and Bagnall locomotives. In Kent, the Sittingbourne-based Bowaters paper mill operation was big enough to have an extensive fleet of Bagnall and Kerr Stuart side and saddle tank locomotives on a significant mileage of railway, requiring 24-hour operation and having its own passenger service. The locos were fitted with electric headlamps and American-style spark arresting chimneys to assist working in the fire risk areas of the paper mills.

Above: In the East Midlands ironstone region, the last narrow gauge railways for extracting ore had in essence standard gauge locomotives slimmed down to fit metre gauge tracks. This is one of three large Peckett saddle tanks now preserved from the Wellingborough system, which closed in 1966. It and its sisters can now be seen at the Irchester Narrow Gauge Railway Museum.

Below: The Bowaters paper mill line in Kent had an industrial system lasting to the end of the 1960s that had its own passenger service. Now preserved at the Sittingbourne & Kemsley Railway, one of the distinctive Bagnall tank engines enters the Sittingbourne station in July 2008 with one of the bespoke passenger coaches behind it.

The Baldwin 4-6-0 side tank is synonymous with the First World War light railways. Built in their hundreds for service on the Western Front, they were dispersed widely at the end of hostilities. The engine in this picture went to a sugar mill in India, returned to the UK in the 1980s and is now based at the Leighton Buzzard Light Railway, but was operating at a First World War commemoration event at the Apedale Railway in September 2014.

Did you know?

In 1953, a flood in Kent saw the Sittingbourne loco *Conqueror* submerged by floodwater. True to its name, the engine was salvaged and ran until the end of the system in commercial use, and is now in preservation, although not yet on display.

The First World War saw an explosion of locomotive demand, and it was a measure of the UK manufacturing capacity that a large number of orders had to go to the USA, where the companies had the capacity to build cheap locomotives quickly. Hunslet of Leeds built a quantity of 2 foot gauge 4-6-0 side tanks, to their usual high standard and quality, but the War Department needed locomotives for the Western Front systems faster than Hunslet could supply them. Baldwin stepped in, and made hundreds of their similar design. At the end of hostilities, these simple and rugged, effective locos found ready homes across the world in a number of new uses. Some remained in use in Indian sugar mills until the 1980s – not bad for a machine with a design life of eighteen months. At home, the steam locomotives were found varied homes, from the Ashover and Snailbeach mineral railways to Harrogate Gasworks and the Glyn Valley Tramway. In the latter case, the rough and ready Baldwin was

Another First World War design was the Hudson 0-6-0 Well tank, made by Hudswell Clarke. Suitable for lightly laid lines, a number found their way to contractors' use in peacetime. The loco in the picture never saw service in conflict but went to the Ashanti Goldfields in Ghana; it was representing its type at the Apedale Railway First World War event 'Tracks to the Trenches' of 2014.

a world apart from the refined Beyer Peacock tram engines which had been operating the line for over thirty years when the new engine arrived. Baldwins remained in use on the Ashover line in Derbyshire until the early 1950s, but were so worn out that no thought to preservation was given at all – the Talyllyn was only beginning its life as a heritage line in 1951 and had yet to prove itself as a viable concept.

The First World War also saw the beginning of petrol-engined loco development – steam locomotives working to the front were very conspicuous, with smoke and steam visible by day and the glare from the firebox and sparks from the chimney at night, so something less noticeable was needed on the supply lines. Steam still worked on the heavier trains to supply centres, but the petrol tractor ran to the battle zone. Some superb film exists of these operations and can be accessed by the internet on https://www.youtube.com/watch?v=vhlm67eLrpI.

In the 1920s the high-pressure enclosed engines and vertical boilers that had been used on road steam waggons from the Sentinel works in Shrewsbury were tried out on a locomotive application. High power, low speed and ease of operation made these almost the final flowering of commercial narrow gauge steam locomotives. A large number of these found use in the brickworks of the London Brick Company around Bedfordshire, the last survivor being *Nutty* from 1929, looking almost like a diesel with enclosed bodywork. It can now be seen at the Leighton Buzzard Narrow Gauge Railway although it is part of the collection of the Narrow Gauge Railway Museum Trust. Articulation was tried in the hope of making such power units more attractive but the influx of cheap internal combustion power in the period

Above: A final flowering of high technology narrow gauge steam came with the Sentinel locomotives built at Shrewsbury. Based on the boiler and engine units of Sentinel steam waggons, they were slow but high powered for their low weight and found use in many applications from quarries to brickworks, the latter being where *Nutty* worked. Now displayed at the Leighton Buzzard Narrow Gauge Railway, it is on loan from the Narrow Gauge Railway Museum collection.

Below: The ultimate narrow gauge locomotive in the UK was Bagnall's articulated locomotive *Monarch*, built for the Sittingbourne system in 1953. While the technology was sound, it wasn't necessarily 100 per cent successful but survived into preservation on the Welshpool & Llanfair Light Railway, where it is on static display.

after the First World War and then the rapid development of the oil and diesel engine meant that in reality, the hold of steam on the UK narrow gauge market was broken. Very few steam locomotives were made for home use after 1930, with a few going to civil engineering jobs, a couple to the slate industry and in the 1950s, a large Bagnall articulated loco, *Monarch*, being made for the Bowaters paper mills at Sittingbourne. By that time, most narrow gauge locos that were produced were for the still lucrative export market – which remained operative though declining until 1971.

The Beyer Garratt articulated locomotive, another approach to the two locomotives in one concept was a purely British idea, the brainchild of Herbert W. Garratt, but in real terms its full potential was met in the export market, very few Garratts being made for the home market, and none to narrow gauge. The type was made right up until 1968, having commenced in 1909, and the majority made were for narrow gauge lines in other countries. Africa made the Garratt its own, and while their working days do not come within the sphere of this book, in heritage use a number of 2 foot gauge Garratts from South Africa have carved a niche for themselves on the revived Welsh Highland Railway. Their light weight and high power, with two engine units and a single boiler, has made them suitable for the sharp curves, steep gradients and heavy trains of the tourist line. For many there is no finer sight than a Garratt pulling up the twisting line from Beddgelert, and while a far cry from the African lines, it is much closer for the UK enthusiast to see an articulated locomotive running on similar terrain to which it was designed for. It is perhaps fitting that the Welsh Highland Railway terminates at Porthmadog Harbour station, on a platform alongside the Ffestiniog Railway, so at certain times of day each summer season, two designs of narrow gauge super-power articulated steam locomotives can be seen alongside each other as Garratt meets Fairlie.

While the Beyer Garratt articulated locomotive was developed in the UK, no narrow gauge locomotives were made for use in the country of their origin. In the preservation era, the very first Garratt came back to the UK and now runs on the Welsh Highland Railway. It appeared in Manchester in 2009 to commemorate its being built there a century previously.

Above: The final development of the Beyer Garratt on the narrow gauge was the NGG16, made for South Africa. The revived Welsh Highland Railway with its gradients and curves is ideal for these engines, and July 2014 saw Garratt No. 87 arriving at Porthmadog, watched by the author's family.
Below: Long lost locomotives have been recreated in recent years, perhaps the most striking being the new build of a Lynton & Barnstaple type tank loco, currently based on the Ffestiniog & Welsh Highland Railway. Several other machines have now been completed or are under construction.

In the 1970s, the seeds of what is now known as the 'new build phenomenon' were sown. While Hunslet turned out what was believed to be their last commercial steam locomotive in 1971, an 0-4-2 saddle tank for Java, less than ten years later a new passenger-hauling double Fairlie was made by the Ffestiniog Railway in its Boston Lodge works. This was a century after the works had built its first double Fairlie, and paved the way for a number of other new build narrow gauge locomotives – the most notable being the recreation of *Taliesin*, the single Fairlie completed by and for the Ffestiniog Railway to an historic design in 1999. After this, it was almost as if the flood gates opened, and there are new build Quarry Hunslet style locos, Kerr Stuart Wrens and a number of others. Minimum gauge Heywood designs proliferate and it has been wonderful to see a new steam locomotive based on the original Kerr Stuart saddle tank on the Corris Railway, and most recently in 2017, a new build Baldwin style Lynton & Barnstaple 2-4-2, *Lyn*. Many of these recent locos are modern locos constructed to look like the original but with alterations to the construction and also improvements to aid their operation and efficiency. *Lyn* looks like the original, but it has the gas producer combustion system, meaning its coal consumption is lower and more effective and its exhaust is much cleaner than the original would have been. Similarly, the Corris Railway in Mid Wales had both its original locomotives sold in 1952 by British Railways to the Talyllyn Railway, where they still operate. Therefore the revitalised Corris Railway has built a new Kerr Stuart locomotive to the design of its original No. 4 and is now busily creating a new Falcon type 0-4-2 in the style of the original locomotives for the line.

The Corris Railway's original locomotives were both sold in 1951 to the Talyllyn Railway. When Corris itself needed a steam loco, they had a replica of their original No. 4 made to the same pattern and this now represents the railway in the twenty-first century.

Large works have been building these engines, yet a number have been and are being built in backyards – many of these have been low cost, small vertical boiler machines, but at least one very detailed Wren is being built in a workshop in West Yorkshire. Whereas once the new build steam locomotive to traditional design was very much seen as out of the reach of most people, one can now order a new four wheeled saddle tank from an engineering firm in the twenty-first century, much as was possible in the latter years of the nineteenth century onwards – and the price is not much more than for a high specification sports car.

Did you know?

A narrow gauge steam locomotive was built for less than £1,000 in 2000! It used a small steam boiler from a laundry, an engine bought for a bargain price and wheels from a small tipper wagon.

If you don't have a lot of money, a narrow gauge steam loco is still a possibility. Chris Parmenter built *Perseverance* to prove that it could be done for less than £1,000. The result appeared at the Ffestiniog Railway Quirks and Curiosities Event in May 2017.

3

Internal Combustion or Infernal Confusion?

Alternatives to steam power for locomotives had been a consideration for many decades. Electric locomotives had begun to be widespread in the late nineteenth century, but required either a live wire or battery cells for traction. Early internal combustion engine-powered locomotives used petrol as their fuel. Soon after Dr Rudolf Diesel patented his first compression ignition engine in 1892, its application for railway propulsion was considered. Progress was slow, however, due to the poor power-to-weight ratio of the early engines, as well as the difficulty inherent in mechanically applying power to multiple driving wheels.

In the UK, the first oil-engined locomotive was actually the world's first, built by Priestman Brothers of Hull in 1894, followed shortly after in 1896 by the first commercial locomotives, a set of six locomotives built by Richard Hornsby of Grantham for Woolwich Arsenal. Ruston Proctor made paraffin-powered locomotives in the first years of the twentieth century, of which a couple of later developments survive in preservation. The subsequent two decades saw great strides made in the development of light commercial locomotives; these were all

Ruston Proctor made some early petrol/paraffin locos to their type ZLH. Of metre gauge, this one dates from 1916 and is in the collection of the Vale of Rheidol Railway at Aberystwyth. Rustons later combined with Richard Hornsby and became major manufacturers of internal combustion locomotives.

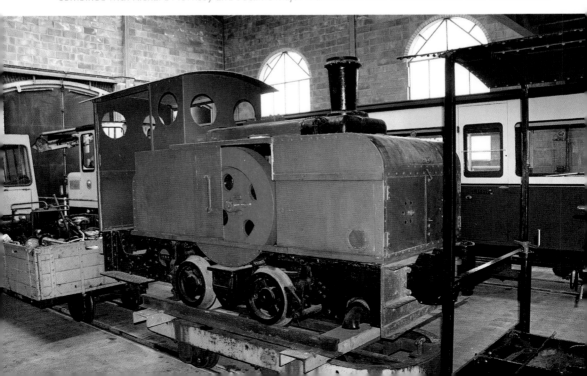

The First World War was really the start of widespread adoption of petrol locomotives across the UK. While the technology saw service in France, it was spread rapidly after the end of hostilities as the military locomotives were sold into civilian service. At the Welsh Highland Heritage Railway museum, a bow frame Simplex loco represents its War Department Light Railway origins.

The petrol locomotives operating at the Front were mainly from Simplex or Baguley, the pioneering manufacturers. Baguleys were less numerous, and not as many have survived – this one had a chequered life after the conflict and was recovered from a chalk pit and is now part of the Welsh Highland Heritage Railway collection. In the photo, it was at the Apedale Railway's 'Tracks to the Trenches' event.

petrol powered and mainly from new players in the railway supply industry who challenged the existing steam locomotive manufacturers. Manufacturers such as Motor Rail & Tramcar, Hibberd, Kent Construction Company, Baguley and a diverse array of others entered the locomotive market and made themselves a name for supplying light engines that could find any number of commercial applications, their initial development having grown out of the First World War, as noted in the last chapter. At the cessation of hostilities, the industrial locomotive market was flooded with these tractors and many were sold for contractors' use as railways were the main way of earthmoving on civil engineering contracts. However, these were in the main very light machines, mainly for shunting and trip work, and unsuitable for main line goods or passenger work on either standard or narrow gauge lines.

As the railways to the Western Front got closer to the fighting, there was need for protecting the loco crews. This varied from simple protection as here to full armour plating. The visibility and noise for the driver were less than ideal, and few survived into the heritage period with the plating intact. This protected example belongs to the Apedale collection but was seen in operation at Beamish Museum in April 2016.

Kerr Stuart pioneer No. 4415, the first British-built diesel mechanical locomotive, stored in the Minffordd goods shed of the Ffestionig Railway in April 2009 pending restoration to working order. It had latterly been on a plinth in Mauritius after a long and varied working life.

Low cost petrol tractors were beginning to dominate the contractors' railway scene with their ability to start almost instantly and having less reliance on long preparation and disposal regimes. They also required fewer people to work on them and the technology was the same as the lorries that worked alongside them, so expensive boiler repairs were avoided. On the narrow gauge and light railways that were ill-placed economically to deal with expensive steam locomotive repairs, petrol railcars were tried, and as the diesel engine itself was developed, thoughts turned to fitting one of these engines into a locomotive, and the late 1920s were noted for several manufacturers trying their hand at this new technology. Large units required an external starting mechanism, be it compressed air, an electric motor or a petrol auxiliary engine. Kerr Stuart were determined to sell this technology in a working locomotive, and had a talented development engineer, Kyrle Willans, who had a background in innovative engineering.

The late 1920s were a time of recession and economic hardship, and many old established engineering firms either struggled or went out of business. Many attempts were made to amalgamate or adapt to ride out the storm, but the decade saw the demise of such firms as Manning Wardle of Leeds, and Kerr Stuart themselves in 1929 – though this was due to a misappropriation of funds by the company chairman.

It was into this world that Kerr Stuart introduced their works number 4415 in 1928 as the first production diesel-powered locomotive in Britain, and the precursor to all subsequent diesel

Baldwin's petrol tractors from the First World War were imported for when the UK deliveries could not cope, and a number survive across the world. The Ffestiniog Railway bought one in 1925, which amazingly they still own to this day. June 2016 saw it operating at Beamish Museum on the narrow gauge system there.

mechanical, diesel electric and diesel hydraulic locos that followed very soon afterwards. It so happened that it was a narrow gauge locomotive, and is massively relevant today, more so in that it survives in preservation at the Ffestiniog and Welsh Highland railways after a career that saw it go from Stoke to Wales to Ireland and Mauritius before returning to Wales in the 1990s.

With internal combustion finding favour, the manufacturers of Baguley, and very much more the Motor Rail & Tram Car Company, developed some really practical and useful four wheel locomotives, often referred to as 'tractors'. The latter's locomotives had the trade name 'Simplex' and were available in open, protected and armoured versions. Upon cessation of hostilities, many of these locomotives were sold into industry and began the death knell of the industrial narrow gauge steam locomotive. Cheap, easy to run and plentiful, a major user of these was the significant sand-carrying railway network around Leighton Buzzard. They quickly dispensed with their two steam locomotives and dozens of Simplex locomotives from war surplus and later construction by the same company became synonymous with the railway for five decades. In addition to the UK-built engines, a number of Baldwin gas/petrol tractors were imported for use on the extensive light railway systems; one of these locomotives survives on the Ffestiniog Railway, where it had been purchased as army surplus in 1925 – showing that internal combustion on narrow gauge public railways is nothing new.

Did you know?

The heaviest Simplex locomotives were the armoured versions and were totally enclosed. They acquired the nickname 'Tin Turtle' on account of their appearance and shuffling movement.

Diesel engine technology improved and grew – the technology allowed crossover with other industrial plant, pumps and tractors. A Lister was light but powerful for its size and could go places where other locomotives couldn't. The rail truck was the ultimate light locomotive and Listers found ready use on temporary lines and light railways across the peat levels in Somerset, Shropshire and elsewhere. Even in the 1980s, when a line was put in at the British Railways Nurseries at Poppleton near York, the resident Simplex loco could not fit on the tracks between greenhouses, so a Lister was borrowed due to its narrowness and flexibility. Ruston & Hornsby, Hudson-Hunslet and Hibberd all entered the market with bespoke designed locomotives, while Muir Hill adapted agricultural tractors and many thousands of similar machines were made across the country. The firm Robert Hudson of Leeds set themselves up as major international suppliers of narrow gauge light and industrial railway equipment, and their regular catalogues became massive hardback publications as time progressed – locomotives being but a small part of their range.

Mines were another area where the diesel locomotive found a niche. Locomotives were required to replace pit ponies underground in collieries. Steam could not be used for fear of igniting gases. Battery electrics were not reliable and third rail or wire electrics could give off sparks in the pick-up process. Petrol locomotives also have spark plugs and could set off any firedamp in the mine. Diesels also could give off hot gases and flames carried through their exhausts when working hard, so innovation was required. In the 1930s, development of the flameproof mines diesel locomotive took place with the manufacturers Hudswell Clarke, North British and Hunslet. The exhaust gases pass through a number of gauzes and filters to ensure that no flames could reach the atmosphere and as a result, diesel locomotives found

At the lightweight end of the spectrum, the Lister Rail Truck was the ultimate where power was required but at as light a weight as possible. A pair of Listers are seen at Twyford Waterworks; one has a roof to at least try and keep the driver dry!

Above: The growth of the small diesel locomotive throughout the 1930s saw many new names enter the locomotive building market, most of whom had not been active with steam. Ruston & Hornsby of Lincoln became major players and hundreds of their products remain today, such as this 20DL type seen at the private Richmond Light Railway in Kent.

Below: The petrol engine lent itself to adaptation and Muir Hill carved a niche for themselves using Fordson tractors as the basis for narrow gauge locomotives. As simple machines they were easily maintained, but very few lasted into preservation. This privately owned example was seen at the Ffestiniog Railway in May 2017.

Above: Underground mine locomotives were a specific application where the diesel locomotive came into its own once the flameproof technology was perfected. One of the oldest survivors is the pioneering Hudswell Clarke loco from 1946, now in the collection of Leeds Museums at Armley Mills, though it is not currently on public display.

Below: Further use of locomotives in mines extended to the development of rack locomotives for steep gradients and smaller shunting locomotives. These two are seen at Middleton Railway in Leeds, and their white livery was to assist with visibility underground.

use in UK coal mines into the twenty-first century. Where gradients were a challenge to normal locomotives, rack and pinion locomotives used cogs with teeth to engage in a central slotted rail – the rack – to climb steeper hills. Hunslet specifically made engines like this and in 1986 used the technology to build new locomotives for the Snowdon Mountain Railway, a tourist attraction whose steam locomotives were ageing and needed support.

Not all diesels were small four or six wheeled devices; the companies of Avonside and Hunslet both made bogie pattern diesels in the 1930s, which articulated the locomotive, very much in the Fairlie pattern of steam locomotives. Avonsides were all exported, while some of Hunslet's production remained in the UK at Woolwich Arsenal on the system there. One of the locos has survived into preservation.

Latterly, internal combustion locomotive production has very much been the preserve of Alan Keef of Ross-on-Wye, who also now own the Simplex name and designs. Baguley of Burton-on-Trent have also made locomotives in recent years, but with the decline of industrial narrow gauge, production has not been large – though reconditioning of older units still continues as well.

There have always been imports of internal combustion locos, initially from the USA and Germany, some single cylinder Deutz engines being utilised in varying industries. Numbers have not tended to be great, though, given the ability of the UK market to satisfy its own needs. As with steam, there have been larger imports of locomotives since the 1980s for preservation and heritage use, and the largest examples of these are the LyD locos from Poland and Funkey Bo-Bos from South Africa, both of which are finding use as alternatives for passenger trains on the various railways that have acquired them.

Very many diesel locomotives have been preserved either as static exhibits or as working machines in the UK, and to a lesser extent in many countries of the world. Definitions of what exactly constitutes a 'preserved' locomotive may vary, however, as a number of 'preserved' locomotives have either been scrapped or sold back into commercial use after a period in the heritage sector. There are several hundred diesel mechanical locomotives in preservation alone in the UK.

Imported internal combustion engines were often found but not hugely widespread. This Deutz single cylinder loco was used in the Welsh slate industry alongside British-built steam, petrol and electric machines.

4
The Spark of Progress – Electric Locomotives

The first known electric locomotive was built in 1837 by chemist Robert Davidson of Aberdeen. It was powered by galvanic cells (batteries). Davidson later built a larger locomotive named *Galvani*, exhibited at the Royal Scottish Society of Arts Exhibition in 1841. The 7-ton vehicle had two direct-drive motors, with fixed electromagnets acting on iron bars attached to a wooden cylinder on each axle, and simple commutators. It hauled a load of 6 tons at 4 miles per hour for a distance of 1½ miles. It was tested on the Edinburgh & Glasgow Railway in September of the following year, but the limited power from batteries prevented its general use. It was destroyed by railway workers, who saw it as a threat to their security of employment.

The first electric passenger train was demonstrated by Werner von Siemens in Berlin in 1879. During four months, the train carried 90,000 passengers on a 300-metre-long circular track. The electricity (150 V DC) was supplied through a third insulated rail between the tracks. In the UK, the first electric passenger line was Volk's Electric Railway, opened in 1883 in Brighton. The second iteration of this railway is of narrow gauge and in operation to this day although, using powered tramcars, it has no locomotives. Much of the early development of electric locomotion was driven by the increasing use of tunnels; electricity quickly became the power supply of choice for underground lines.

Development continued in Europe, where electrification was widespread, with the North Eastern Railway putting in DC lines in Newcastle for commuters and the quayside in 1904. The same company electrified the main line from Shildon to Newport for coal traffic in 1915 and a number of other DC systems were developed in the UK. It was against this growing use of electric power that the scene was being set for the use of electric locomotives in industry – and a number were built for use in power stations, collieries and other systems where instant availability and cleanliness were attractive advantages. The electrification of aspects of industry paved the way for the new power to find application in locomotives as well as plant on site. This is where narrow gauge comes in, as the story of main line electrification takes a much greater importance in terms of the complexity of the history – and it's just as well, as this book is certainly not big enough to take everything into account.

Did you know?

George Stephenson (early railway and steam locomotive pioneer and engineer) was shown the principles of electric traction later in life, and reckoned it would be the ultimate form of propulsion. He is reputed to have said words to the effect of 'develop that ... much better than tinkering with steam engines'.

There are a few hundred electric locomotives in preservation in the UK; most of these are narrow gauge battery electrics built for mining, tunnelling or contractors' firms. Early electric locomotives are rare and conversions of steam locomotives into electrics are confined to the two machines that fit into our 'Odd Ones Out' chapter.

The panoply of electric locomotives is reflected on the narrow gauge in that examples of third rail, battery and overhead wire electricity supply have all been used, and to a certain extent, all are represented in preservation today. Electricity finds special use in places where steam and diesel could not meet requirements, due to its cleanliness – and one of the most extreme cases of swords into ploughshares exits in the electric narrow gauge locomotive. In the latter part of the First World War, Brush made electric locomotives for the Avonmouth mustard gas factory. Upon cessation of hostilities, like so much war surplus, the equipment found new use, and the railway was sold to form the basis of the Hythe Pier Tramway in Hampshire, carrying passengers and luggage to a ferry terminal using third rail electric pick-up, being converted from battery power. The railway still runs today, with the original

100 years old and still going strong. The Brush electric locomotives built for the Avonmouth mustard gas factory found peacetime use on the Hythe Pier Tramway in Hampshire and are still operating today.

Emphasising how small electric locomotives can be, this Greenwood & Batley four-wheeled machine is now preserved at the Ripon & District Light Railway, where the photograph was taken in November 2017.

English Electric/Dick Kerr built three locomotives for the underground Post Office Railway in Central London. While the line no longer runs commercially, the locos remain for the heritage attraction, but this example was seen in March 2005 while the line was mothballed and a decision on its future was awaited.

One of the oldest electric locomotives in the UK other than the Avonmouth machines is the British Electric Vehicles 0-4-0, which was once employed and displayed at Llechwedd Slate Caverns and is now owned by Patrick Keef. It was in the Llechwedd Museum on their site in the 1980s.

The narrow gauge new-build phenomenon extends to the non-steam world and the short-lived electric locomotives on the Groudle Glen Railway on the Isle of Man have been recreated using a 1980s Wingrove & Rogers locomotives as a basis.

equipment, and the locomotives are now a century old. Third rail electricity was also the power behind the Post Office Railway, which ran an extensive fleet of driverless parcel trains for over 6 miles under London streets until 2003 in an intensive operation. Now reopened as a tourist attraction, the line runs with modern battery electric units, though most of the original trains remain either stored or on display. A trio of English Electric battery locomotives are kept, originally for use when the third rail was turned off for maintenance but now as historic pieces of equipment.

The concept of electric traction is of course nothing new, and less than two years after the North Eastern Railway pioneered main line electric locomotives on Tyneside, the Porthmadog, Beddgelert & South Snowdon Railway was planning the creation of its line using electricity from the outset. The tunnels through Aberglaslyn Pass were built to the appropriate loading gauge to allow for overhead cables and a batch of locomotives were ordered from Bruce Peebles & Co., and construction undertaken. Ultimately the scheme fell through, the line was never finished, at least not by the PB&SSR, and the locomotives were scrapped as there was no other use for them in the UK. Their Ganz technology became outdated and the world moved on to the next great project. Ironically, the route of the railway became the Welsh Highland Railway, which finally opened in the early 1920s and incorporated the North Wales Narrow Gauge Railway, which met the PB&SSR.

Battery locomotives are where the power found its greatest application on the narrow gauge, due to the small size that battery locomotives could be made to. Mining, tunnelling and civil engineering made and still do make great use of these locomotives – thousands being constructed and most being under the radar of the world at large, due to their quietly getting on with business on construction sites or deep under the earth. Some manufacturers of these locomotives never built steam or diesel engines, but have been the most successful builders in their field, Greenwood & Batley, Wingrove & Rogers and British Electric Vehicles (BEV) being the main players, while Clayton Equipment in Derby continue to build battery electric locomotives for mining and engineering into the twenty-first century. Electric mines locos saw out the final production at Ellington colliery in Northumberland and rubber-tyred battery electrics, of the Clayton 'Pony' type, were some of the last locomotives in the final UK deep coal mine, Kellingley in Yorkshire, which wound its last coal in December 2015.

Changing batteries on an electric locomotive is an operation that is not often seen. The work was captured a few years ago on the now closed Miners' Tramway at the Llechwedd Slate Caverns in Blaenau Ffestiniog. The size of the batteries and their weight is apparent!

One of the last working narrow gauge locomotives in the Welsh slate industry was the 1974-built Clayton electric locomotive from Aberllefenni quarry near Corris; it operated until 2007 and the closure of the quarry. Now preserved at the Corris Railway, it is ideal for shunting operations and was seen delivering the wagons for a gravity train in June 2017.

Underground electric locomotives are not just small machines for man-riding purposes; some large bogie locos were made. Clayton of Derby also made this 1980s loco, now used at the National Coal Mining Museum for England, where it's part of the passenger ride offered around the site. It was awaiting duty when photographed on 21 July 2014.

Small mines locos lend themselves to preservation in a variety of locations. August 2017 found this Wingrove & Rogers on display at Allenheads in Cumbria, commemorating the mining industry of the region's past.

5
The Odd Ones Out

In this chapter, we consider the locomotives that don't find a place in any of the previous chapters. Neither one thing nor the other, for years enthusiasts and historians have tended to overlook them as unconventional and hard to understand. By putting them in this section, we can value them for their true worth and set them in context for what they really are – valuable pieces of transport and engineering heritage in their own right.

We start with the two steam locomotives converted to overhead electric engines. As such, their working lives extended far beyond what they would have been had they remained steam powered. The two 1 ft 11⅝ in. gauge locomotives, *The Eclipse* and *The Coalition*, were built for and have remained with the Welsh slate quarrying industry all their lives. Both were originally constructed as Bagnall steam locomotives and were subsequently modified to overhead wire electric propulsion very early on in the development of electric traction for railways. They are very good examples of the resourcefulness shown by industrial users who converted existing equipment for reuse in significantly different form.

Both locomotives were converted from steam to electric traction by the same method under the direction of Captain Martyn Williams-Ellis of J. W. Greaves Ltd. The electrical equipment package was supplied by General Electric Co. Ltd (GEC). As the first electric locomotives to be constructed in Wales, they have an extra significance and are most unusual, for the locomotive building industry in Wales has been very small.

The 1927 conversions of Bagnall steam locos to electric locomotives at Llechwedd slate quarry were ground-breaking and innovative. The work extended the operating lives of the two locomotives into the 1970s and has ensured their survival into preservation. Here's *The Eclipse* at the quarry in the 1990s; it has since moved to store pending a restoration plan.

Spooner's Boat on the Ffestiniog Railway is unique in being both sail and gravity powered. Here it coasts downhill to Tanygrisiau station during a vintage weekend in October 2011.

The conversion was described in detail in a contemporary article in *Modern Traction for the Industrial and Agricultural Railways*. Williams-Ellis also produced a booklet, *Electric Traction as Applied to Quarries & Mines*, which was published around 1927–28, referring to the locomotives and quarry equipment. In converted form, the locomotives continued to work commercially well into the 1970s, being withdrawn when the narrow gauge rail traffic ceased within the Llechwedd mills. Since this time, *The Eclipse* and *The Coalition* remained on static display within the Quarry Tours complex until recent display at the Welsh Highland Heritage Railway in 2010.

Fully rigged, Spooner's Boat was on display in Minffordd Yard during the 2017 Quirks and Curiosities 2 event. Truly a sight to see!

The challenge of their future restoration and interpretation remains; some enthusiasts and historians feel that the locomotives should be returned to steam power.

Spooner's Boat is another oddity, and while not unique in the UK it was a rare wind-powered rail vehicle. With sail aloft, the Spooner family were able to travel independently along the Ffestiniog Railway in late Victorian times. It did have to be turned by hand at the end of each trip.

Did you know?

The Boat met its end when, on one outing, it met a double Fairlie locomotive and train going the other way, the Boat's crew having ignored the rules for single line working. While there were injuries, the passengers recovered after a few days in bed, it is reported.

Another form of 'wind' power on the narrow gauge was the compressed air locomotive. A number of these were made in the UK, mostly being built for use in the mining industry during the nineteenth century. Lishman & Young of Durham were major builders, though they made no other locomotives of conventional type, and a full size replica of one of their engines from 1888 was built in 2009 by Roy Etherington and the team at Statfold Barn Railway. In contrast, although it did not work in the UK, an EIMCO compressed air

Nearly 100 years of compressed air locomotive technology is here in this image from May 2017. On the left is the replica Lishman & Young *Issin Sid*, and on the right the Eimco *Whistling Pig*; the latter is attached to a compressor for charging via the hose connected to it.

locomotive from 1968 is preserved on the Lea Bailey Light Railway in the Forest of Dean. It and the Lishman & Young replica appeared together at the 2017 Ffestiniog Railway 'Quirks and Curiosities' event.

The world of locomotive development is full of unusual beasts. In the volatile industries such as timber, gunpowder and paper, sparks and flames from locomotives were perpetual hazards. In the paper industry, the extensive narrow gauge railway at Lloyd's mills at Sittingbourne had a Bagnall fireless steam locomotive. Quite appropriately named *Unique*, it certainly was on the narrow gauge at least, being a conventional locomotive running gear but with a steam reservoir instead of a normal boiler. Charged with steam from the mill's static source, it would run for a number of hours before it would need to be recharged. It survives to this day as a static exhibit on the preserved Sittingbourne & Kemsley Railway.

For a railway or industry to invest in a locomotive, it's a fairly major decision to spend capital on buying a new or second-hand machine. Over the decades, a number of industries, railways and individuals have made their own engine on the grounds of cost or practicality. The steam home builds for pleasure have already been noted, but the internal combustion and electric locomotives have been many and varied. Some have been extremely professional, and the Morris conversions of cars for Penrhyn Quarry might be considered thus. At the other end of the spectrum comes the motorised skip, plank or re-purposed electric milk float. The Lincolnshire potato railways saw a variety of home-built motive power, and even recently, old locomotives have been rebuilt with other power sources – new air-cooled engines and bodywork for example. The narrow gauge has never been short of ingenuity!

Despite being called *Unique*, this Bagnall fireless loco at Sittingbourne was once accompanied by a second of its type. Now in preservation, it is the only survivor, and was on static display at Kemsley Down in July 2008.

Home-built locomotives could be complex or simple affairs. Conversions of cars were commonplace, as this loco, which used to be on display at Llechwedd Slate Caverns, and was based on a Morris, shows.

6
Twenty-First Century Narrow Gauge

Narrow gauge is so often associated with old and quaint that it is important to remember that this type of railway remains a useful industrial enterprise in the twenty-first century. In 2000, there were still a number of large commercial applications for narrow gauge outside the heritage sector. In the main, these were mining, civil engineering and the Post Office. Far from rustic byways, these arteries of industry moved thousands of tons of spoil during projects such as the Channel Tunnel or Crossrail, and could move men and coal under the North Sea faster than the conveyor systems first introduced. Until 2003, mail was moved around the city of London beneath the streets across 6 miles or more at 40 miles an hour without drivers. Steam power is a thing of the past and diesel and electric reign. The last deep coal mines to use narrow gauge locomotives closed in 2015 but loco power remains in use at some of the small independent collieries using adit access to the seam, especially in Cumbria.

Should you wish to buy a locomotive, there is a thriving trade in second-hand machines, sometimes through plant and machinery auction sales, or dealers. Otherwise, one can turn

If you want narrow gauge locos built or repaired, one of the major companies in the UK is Alan Keef Ltd of Ross-on-Wye. On occasion the company runs open days in aid of the local church and in September 2009, a new build De Winton replica was in steam on the mixed-gauge test track along with a newly overhauled Jung 0-4-0 tank loco.

Above: Until 2014, horticultural peat was still being extracted on an industrial scale in Cumbria. An extensive narrow gauge system at Bolton Fell was run intensively to keep up with demand. A fleet of Simplex locos provided the power, and some of these dated from the 1930s although they had been re-engined and brought up to date. In this picture, a number of trains await loading out on the moss.
Below: Trackwork on the peat railways was basic!

to new build from specialists such as Alan Keef, who do industrial and pleasure line work, or Severn Lamb, who solely deal in pleasure railway operations. Keef's have a vibrant works in the Forest of Dean, repairing, overhauling and building steam, diesel and electric locomotives – and even have a range of their own new build locomotives, having constructed over eighty since the 1970s. Unusually for an industry, the business is very open to enthusiasts and holds regular open days for charity when projects are available to view and enjoy. Given the international scope of the company, this can be very interesting.

A further use of commercial narrow gauge until 2014 was in the peat extraction business. Due to the nature of peat bogs, road transport was not a practical proposition, so the light construction and ease of laying of narrow gauge made it ideal for lines out onto

The height of narrow gauge diesel locomotive development was seen in the Hunslet diesels built for man-riding on underground colliery systems. Less than twenty years old when this picture was taken at Ellington Colliery, the Hunslet closest to the camera was designed to take men 7 miles to the coal face faster than they could ride the conveyor belt. The loco is now part of the collection at Bowes Railway, Springwell, near Gateshead.

the moss. 2 foot gauge and 3 foot gauge were the usual sizes and some major brands of peat moss sold at garden centres began life on narrow gauge railways in South Yorkshire, Cumbria and Scotland. Locomotives were Rustons, Simplexes and a few Keefs, and latterly some Schomas on the mosses around Doncaster. On the Bolton Fell workings in Cumbria, a fleet of 1930s Simplexes with modern air-cooled power units were merrily hard at work over several shifts a day. Delivering to a rotary tippler for onward processing, all came to an end in June 2014 due to a Government ruling and the railway was removed the following month. I was fortunate to visit the line twice, and it was an amazing system to one so used to the heritage scene. Curves were almost non-existent, the rails were laid at angles to each other and the track was laid on membranes to carry the weight across the surface of the peat bog. Trains were intensive with at least six locomotives in use at one time.

January 2005 saw the last operations of locomotives at Ellington Colliery in Northumberland, out of Bewick Drift yard on 3 foot gauge, though rail use for clearance finally ceased in April 2005. The rails extended up to 7 miles out under the North Sea, and modern Hunslet diesel hydraulic locomotives were used – bogie machines with a cab at each end and able to travel at 25 miles an hour for man-riding duties out to the working face. Some of these were less than twenty years old at the closure. Alongside these were more traditional mines diesels from the 1950s and 1960s of the 0-6-0 flameproof single cab design by Hudswell Clarke, used for materials and maintenance movements as coal was sent out on conveyor belting. In my capacity for work, I went to the site to select a locomotive for preservation in the National Collection, choosing one of the latter – the very final locomotive out of the workings.

Did you know?

The final locomotive out of Ellington Colliery had it's driver's name and service dates written in the cab and 'The Last Train at Big E' written in marker pen on the side. A very poignant record indeed.

One of the last drivers at Ellington colliery made his mark in April 2005. The message remains on the locomotive, which is now displayed at Locomotion in Shildon, County Durham.

The final word!

The largest civil engineering project of the twentieth century, the Channel Tunnel, used narrow gauge railways, and civil engineering continues to use the technology on major works. In London, the Crossrail project has seen many contractors' locomotives and wagons as the narrow gauge railway has yet to be improved upon in this application. A number of major plant contractors still have fleets of diesel and electric locomotives, as do tunnelling engineers. From time to time, these machines break cover on a building site or occasionally at an auction of plant, where they are viewed as something different among the generators and JCB excavators. Narrow gauge railways still remain a practical part in the industrial economy of the UK, albeit on a smaller scale than a century ago.

The use of narrow gauge railways by the military also continued into the twenty-first century, with the last system being at Eastriggs in southern Scotland, not far from Gretna, where the munitions factory had an internal line in the First World War. The network at Eastriggs was extensive and even had a dual gauge locomotive shed for both narrow gauge and standard gauge engines. The Ministry of Defence had invested in a standard type of narrow gauge locomotive in the late 1980s, all Barclay-built diesel mechanical locomotives that also had the facility to be used as mobile power generators and compressors, allowing tools to be used out at remote locations on the track. Operations at Eastriggs finished in 2014, with all equipment being sold to heritage venues.

Mining and tunnelling remain the most extensive users of narrow gauge railway equipment in the twenty-first century. While the Channel Tunnel opened in the 1990s, the locomotive and rubble car displayed at the National Railway Museum are representative of the dozens of locos working on projects such as Crossrail across the country.

Relatively modern narrow gauge locomotives are useful commodities. When these 1985-built locomotives were made redundant at Shotton steelworks, they found a new home at the Welsh Highland Railway as operational machines rather than preserved pieces of heritage. As late build Hunslets, they retain an interest that will only increase over time.

The Ministry of Defence continued to use narrow gauge until 2013, the final system remaining being at Eastriggs depot in south-west Scotland. A number of state of the art Barclay diesels were built in the 1980s for use across the MoD; the last five of these were concentrated at Eastriggs by February 2013, when this photo was taken in the mixed-gauge locomotive shed – where a standard gauge shunter can just be seen behind the Barclays.

Did you know?

MoD Eastriggs had five narrow gauge/standard gauge crossings in less than a hundred metres.

If a railway working for a living is commercial, then some of the pleasure lines of the last forty years can fit into this area rather than heritage. Tourist attractions, garden centres and festivals have all had railways which have been capable of moving large numbers of people, either as a pleasure ride such as at the Cotswold Wildlife Park or Blists Hill Museum or as a means to moving visitors around a site, as has been the case at the Glasgow Garden Festival and Whipsnade Zoo – where spare locomotives from the Kent Bowaters system found a new use. Two major companies exist for the provision of these railways: Alan Keef of Ross-on-Wye and Severn Lamb of Warwickshire. Both will build and equip railways to any specification, with Keef's working on industrial and contractor railways and equipment too. In terms of engineering, the contract work of other workshops such as the Vale of Rheidol Railway and the Statfold Barn operation in Staffordshire are also key players. All cross over into heritage operations and restorations too of a very high standard.

The world of heritage railways has seen new builds, new railways and also the import of many narrow gauge locomotives. Steam locomotives built in Britain for use across the world have been brought back to their place of manufacture for restoration and operation on preserved railways. They illustrate just how far the UK export market for locomotives went, and enrich the historic element of the lines they run on and collections they are shown in as well as being useful pieces of equipment in their own right.

Twenty-first-century narrow gauge is summed up for me in this photo from May 2017 of a heritage train on the Ffestiniog Railway. The locomotive dates from 1999 and is a rebuild of single Fairlie *Taliesin,* and it is leaving a heavily developed Porthmadog Harbour station, but the ethos of the narrow gauge railway as it has been for over a century and a half remains and endures.

In recent years, the Post Office Railway, which ceased commercial operations in 2003 with English Electric third rail units and Greenwood & Batley locomotives, has been revitalised and equipped with Severn Lamb passenger trains. Now able to carry passengers rather than post, it reopened as a tourist attraction in the summer of 2017. Narrow gauge is alive and well and earning a living in the United Kingdom, albeit on a smaller scale than it once was.

Under Central London, the Post Office Railway ran for 6 miles, operating commercially until May 2003. It was mothballed and placed into store after that, but reopened in part as a tourist venture in 2017. A visit to the railway in March 2005 found driverless electric unit No. 25 stored at Mount Pleasant station.

7
What Now?

The narrow gauge railway has held a fascination of its own for decades. Marketed by many in the early twentieth century as 'quaint' or 'toy' railways, the commercial common carrier narrow gauge line was in real terms a butterfly. It blossomed for a while then sank into quick decline and very few made it intact into the second part of the twentieth century. Its very appeal was its saviour as it ran into danger of extinction so quickly. The first attempt to save a narrow gauge railway was the effort to resurrect the Southwold Railway in Suffolk in the 1930s, but this came to naught and thus it was the heritage pioneer Tom Rolt and the saving of the Talyllyn Railway in Mid Wales that blazed the trail.

Over all the spheres of interest, the umbrella body has to be the Narrow Gauge Railway Society, NGRS for short. Established in 1951, the same year as the Talyllyn Railway re-opened with volunteers, it has become the go-to organisation for anyone with an interest in railways under standard gauge. At one time it collected artefacts and locomotives, but has settled down to collect information, publications, archives and images now. It has a healthy activities programme with visits and publishes widely. http://www.ngrs.org/

Pleasure Park lines
Narrow gauge in Britain has a great adaptability and a propensity to surprise. A significant number of lines exist in pleasure parks, zoos and seaside locations. Their sole purpose is to move visitors around attractions, not always from place to place, sometimes round in circles, and locomotives have been specifically designed for that application. Best known were the Baguleys for Butlins and Alton Towers, petrol and diesel locomotives with a nod to steam outline. Many railway enthusiasts dismiss these lines, with their sole commercial purpose, but delving into their history is a rich and rewarding process. Next time the family goes to a zoo, have a look to see if they have a railway!

Did you know?

The Butlins Railway at Clacton featured in the closing title sequences of the BBC comedy series *Hi-de-Hi* in the 1980s.

The pleasure park railway is an introduction to narrow gauge for all the family, built for fun and sometimes with the aim of moving people around an attraction. The railway at Whipsnade Zoo is one from the 1970s. This uses steam locomotives from the Bowaters system in Kent and was seen not long after opening in this photo.

Heritage Railways

The Talyllyn Railway in Mid Wales blazed the trail for narrow gauge preservation in 1951, being the first railway in the world to be run entirely by volunteers. It was followed shortly afterwards by the Ffestiniog Railway, and the movement grew throughout the 1950s on both an organised and private basis. The main common carrier lines in England, such as the Leek & Manifold and Lynton & Barnstaple railways, had gone before the Second World War. In 1950, the Ashover Railway clung to life as a mineral carrier, but any thoughts of preservation were just those. Only in Wales was action taken to do something, setting the mould for what would follow. Individuals began to save locomotives, a pioneer being Bernard Latham of Woking, who later wrote of his escapades in his book *Railways & Preservation*, including an account of one of his collection demolishing his wife's flowerbed after repair work. Another locomotive, Kerr Stuart *Pixie*, was kept at the back of a pub, and by the 1960s private preservation was well established alongside mainstream heritage railways. The light and simple nature of narrow gauge gives it wider appeal and also means that it can be placed even in an average suburban garden. In the main, it is the 2 foot gauge that has the greatest following and survival of artefacts, also reflecting on the number of lines and the ease of transport by which locomotives can be moved from one site to another. This latter consideration has of course meant that record keeping of a locomotive's location can be fraught with uncertainties!

In Leicestershire, the vicar of Cadeby, Teddy Boston, bought a Bagnall saddle tank and built a line for it around the rectory garden in 1962. Around the same time, Arthur and Hylbert Smith of Oldberrow in Warwickshire had a similar Bagnall saddle tank from the Minworth Sewage Works, which they named *Lady Luxborough*. The Smiths ran it down the drive of where they lived, but with a group of local enthusiasts, including my father, they also took it around steam rallies and other local events, where it was billed as 'The largest portable railway in the world'. Eventually this got too much like hard work and the team

Left: The driver's side view from *Dolgoch* on the Talyllyn Railway.
Below: Volunteering, and helping out on a preservation scheme, is a practical way to get involved. The first railway in the world to be saved by volunteers is the Talyllyn, preserved in 1951 and still operating in 2018. The author is a fireman on the line and took this photo looking up the railway from the footplate in July 2016. Is there any better view in the world?

The ultimate portable railway? For several years in the 1960s, the author's father and friends took Arthur and Hylbert Smith's Bagnall *Lady Luxborough* around steam fairs and events in the Midlands. For the 400th anniversary of Shakespeare's birth, a line was put down alongside the River Avon and happy passengers are seen enjoying their day in Stratford-upon-Avon in 1964.

discovered miniature railways, traction engines and other distractions. *Lady Luxborough* now works at the Bredgar & Wormshill Railway in Kent as *Armistice*. This is a private line with public open days, much in the spirit of the Oldberrow Light Railway where it began its heritage life. Others, such as the Richmond Light Railway, also in Kent, has one annual open day, while in Yorkshire the Ripon Light Railway can be visited by appointment and has a very comprehensive website: www.riponlightrailway.co.uk

The preservation of narrow gauge locomotives crossed over into petrol and diesel machines from the 1960s, and eventually electric locomotives too. Much less expensive to buy and maintain, a plethora of back garden and larger railway schemes grew and some rather large collections ensued, perhaps the largest being that of Rich Morris, Michael Jacob and Peter Nicholson. This latterly became the Narrow Gauge Railway Centre at Gloddfa Ganol Mountain Tourist Centre at Blaenau Ffestiniog in North Wales. Subsequently dispersed in 1997, it was perhaps the largest collection at the time, though in recent years some other long-established lines and museum collections must come close, if not exceeding the number of locomotives on their sites. A few years ago, a small narrow gauge diesel could be bought for not much over £1,000 in working order, and many people bought one, two, three or more to run in fields, in back gardens and around yards. A number of small narrow gauge lines operate as adjuncts to standard gauge heritage lines, such as Peak Rail and the Tanfield Railway. At the latter, the atmosphere is charmingly rustic, as the line weaves its way around the edge of the main loco yard, through ash heaps and round standard gauge wagons. The chance to get involved with all of these and similar lines as a volunteer is universal and the welcome very warm, whether one knows anything about railways or not. I've spent part of most summers since 1990 on the footplate on the Talyllyn Railway, and while I may be biased, there's nothing to beat it.

Above: A personal connection with narrow gauge railways was the Umberslade Light Railway in the garden of Jack Marshall in Hockley Heath. The Marshalls were next door neighbours of my great aunts and latterly grandparents, and Dad was involved with the steam scene in Hockley Heath – so the railway featured massively in my childhood. The loco *Oddson* was made by Jack and friends out of a number of different parts: a vertical boiler, a steam winch and the wheels and frames of a Simplex petrol loco.

Left: Private collections can get out of hand – in which case you open to the public! Rich Morris and friends did just that at Gloddfa Ganol in Blaenau Ffestiniog, which operated from the 1970s to the 1990s. An eclectic mix of locomotives were housed there, as can be seen by this photo from 1992.

Above: It was only a matter of time before a narrow gauge line was laid at Gloddfa Ganol, and this opened in 1987 using former Severn Trent Simplex locos from the Minworth Sewage Works. The line ran from a visitor centre to the narrow gauge collection at the former Oakley Quarry but closed in 1997 when the attraction was sold.

Right: Narrow gauge railways can grow up as adjuncts to established heritage railways – as here at the Tanfield Railway in Tyne & Wear, where a small collection of narrow gauge rolling stock is operated for demonstration purposes at special events.

Museums

When the Talyllyn Railway was in its infancy as a heritage operation, a number of locomotives and artefacts from other closed or closing narrow gauge lines were gathered together at Tywyn Wharf station, and this formed the nucleus of the Narrow Gauge Railway Museum in 1956. Your author was privileged to be a Trustee of the Museum for a decade or so, and was able to be part of the extensive remodelling and display of the museum as it now stands. Unusual gauges and disappeared railways are represented in the collection, and items too large for the site at Tywyn are displayed elsewhere in the country. Some have even been restored to working order at the North Ings Farm Museum in Lincolnshire, where a Ruston and Simplex diesel are used on railway experience days for young enthusiasts to gain experience of running a railway while they are too young to get involved on the Talyllyn itself.

Not long after Tywyn came a museum collection of industrial narrow gauge material at Brockham in Surrey, which later moved to Amberley Chalk Pits in Sussex to become part of the Chalk Pits Museum, with operating line, display hall and a fine collection of steam, internal combustion and electric locomotives.

The National Railway Museum in York was created too late to really cover narrow gauge in depth, having opened in 1975, but it does display a Double Fairlie locomotive, *Livingston Thompson*, on loan from the Ffestiniog Railway, as well as two locomotives from the Crewe and Horwich works systems, plus an electric loco from the Channel Tunnel construction in the 1990s. The NRM's other site, Locomotion in County Durham, displays a Hudswell Clarke

Galas and festivals are regular features of the narrow gauge scene, often to commemorate an anniversary. The Talyllyn Railway's locomotive *Dolgoch* was 150 in 2016, so there was a gathering of all the UK-based survivors of the products of Fletcher Jennings, *Dolgoch*'s builders. Three are seen here at Tywyn Wharf, two narrow gauge locos contrasting with their standard gauge cousin.

mines loco, which was the last locomotive out of Ellington Colliery in Northumberland in April 2005 – the final colliery in the North East of England.

Some narrow gauge lines have become museums in their own right, not just having a museum at a station. Perhaps the first to go down this route was the Leighton Buzzard Narrow Gauge Railway, which has been operating as a heritage line for over fifty years. Initially the passenger trains shared the tracks with the industrial sand trains which used the lines during the week, but they have endured and the whole railway is now classed as an accredited museum – remaining true to its origins, but also reflecting the wider nature of narrow gauge.

Theming is also important. The Leeds Industrial Museum at Armley Mills reflects the very rich locomotive-building legacy of that city and its importance globally, plus also the development of the underground mines diesel locomotive by Hunslet and Hudswell Clarke. The mines locomotive itself is celebrated still further by the massive collection of locos at the Astley Green Colliery Museum in Lancashire.

Beamish Open Air Museum in County Durham have built a new narrow gauge railway in the years since 2010 and demonstrate it with locomotives based on site and to visitors to a number of the special events held at the museum each year. In 2017, for example, the railway was used to move timber around the site between two saw benches powered by steam traction engines. One of the locomotives was the Kerr Stuart *Diana*, built for forestry work in Mid Wales and then latterly used in the slate industry. It was the first time the locomotive had worked on timber trains since its time on the Kerry Tramway. Alongside it was Beamish Museum's own new build Lewin type locomotive *Samson*, finished in 2016 and based on a similar locomotive for the lead mining industry in Weardale. Reflecting non-steam power, the National Railway Museum's 'protected' Simplex diesel loco is now based here. In other years, the railway has moved crushed stone for road making demonstrations and great plans continue for its development as Beamish grows.

Working displays are also a major feature of the railway at Threlkeld Mining Museum in Cumbria, where a steeply graded line climbs from an original locomotive shed to the quarry and

Recreating the past. Ten years ago, there was no narrow gauge railway at Beamish Museum; by April 2015, when this picture was taken, a permanent line was in place and being extended. Not being used for passenger carrying, the line demonstrates the use of narrow gauge railways in industry. Here the Gully family's new build Wren loco *Jennie*, built in 2005, is in use ferrying crushed brick and stone for the author's diesel road roller to roll as hardcore for a railway expansion project.

The April 2017 Beamish Museum event saw the narrow gauge railway celebrating timber haulage and processing, serving two steam-powered saw benches – one to cut long timber and the other to cut short pieces. The Hayward family's Marshall traction engine waits while John Young and Matt Ellis unload the timber bolsters. At the head of the train is Phil Mason's Kerr Stuart loco *Diana*, built 100 years previously to work on timber extraction in Mid Wales.

In Cumbria, a recent narrow gauge heritage development has been the rebuild of the railway system at Threlkeld Quarry near Keswick. This has included bringing the old loco shed back into use, and annual steam galas with themes are held. July 2015's gala had a Penrhyn Quarry feel, with Hunslet *Lilla* and Avonside *Marchlyn* among the star visitors.

A major player in the last two decades has been the Statfold Barn Railway on the Staffordshire/Warwickshire border. What began as a private garden railway has grown into one of the premier collections of narrow gauge locomotives in the country, with regular open days. The accent is on restoration and operation, and part of the collection is shown here in the multi-gauge roundhouse for a society visit in November 2016.

displays are given of loading trains by machines owned on site by the Vintage Excavators Trust. A very fine collection of steam, diesel and electric locomotives are housed here and an annual railway gala complements the earthmover working weekends – truly an experience to savour.

Perhaps the ultimate narrow gauge collections are the Statfold Barn Railway and the nascent Vale of Rheidol Railway Museum. The former grew out of a private garden railway laid down in 2003–4 and now is able to steam almost twenty locomotives on its open days. With a mixed-gauge roundhouse, its collection spans UK-built locomotives built for home and overseas use, as well as a number of Continental locomotives, many brought back from Javanese sugar plantations. Among these is the last commercially built Hunslet, the saddle tank from 1971. A similarly varied collection will form the nucleus of the Vale of Rheidol display, created from a number of locomotives brought together over five decades, once again from all corners of the earth. Truly a golden age for the narrow gauge as new developments are eagerly awaited, though so many locomotives have been imported for preservation since the 1960s, it is beyond the scope of this book to do more than touch on the subject!

Modelling

If the appeal of the narrow gauge inspires you to recreate it at home, many models are available – far more now than at any time and in a dizzying variety of scales and gauges. Inside the home, you can model from N scale up to what is known as 16 mm scale, which then can cross over into the garden, where narrow gauge modelling also comes into its own with the possibility of using real live steam locomotives. From here, it is but a short leap to miniature model locomotives, the type you can ride behind. It's possible not just to build your own locomotive, but if time and skill evade you www.maxitrak.co.uk will build and sell you one of their ready-made locomotives, either steam, petrol or electric powered. As the models get larger, they are almost narrow gauge locomotives in their own right, capable of hard work pulling loads of passengers far in excess of what the prototype would have been expected to do. Back in the domestic environment, the scales of 0 and 00 dominate, with a burgeoning industry of kits to build, ready-to-lay track being available and 3D printed products aplenty. In 00 – or 4 mm scale – locomotives and rolling stock in ready to run format to UK narrow gauge outline are becoming more available, the first of these being the classic Lynton & Barnstaple Railway Manning Wardle 2-6-2s and the Ward Department Baldwin 4-6-0 tank engines. This is known as 009 scale, and the 0 scale version is called 0.16.5 – each has their own society, specialising in advice, kits, drawings, sales and high-quality journals.

Modelling narrow gauge railways can be a cause to indulge your imagination or model a real place – there's room for both! In the case of the latter, sometimes people build models of locations that no longer exist – this 009 scale model is an example, portraying parts of the long-gone Ashover Light Railway.

Above: If one hankers for live steam, narrow gauge models in the garden are a possibility. On the Elmdon Heath Light Railway in the West Midlands, my 16 mm scale steam tram engine has a run out – with a boiler fuelled by methylated spirit, the engine was one of our more unusual wedding presents!

Below: Going larger still, here's a 5 inch gauge Quarry Hunslet working on a temporary line at Tywyn Wharf station in July 2015. These live steam models are large enough to pull people but small enough to fit in a car boot – the best of both worlds!

Models or toys? Or both? This display of model Talyllyn trains was mounted at the 150th anniversary of the railway celebrations and the large scale models were made by a member of the railway for his young son.

Websites and Publications

It may be that none of this is for you, but a number of magazines and websites, plus Youtube channels, cater for the narrow gauge enthusiast, as well as one or two excellent and dedicated Facebook pages. Away from the virtual world, the printed word on narrow gauge railways has been around for around eight decades and shows no sign of abating. This book is very much a primer, an introduction. Should you wish to know more, there are hundreds if not thousands of books on narrow gauge railways. Basic research back in the 1950s paved the way for modern authors and it seems that hardly a month goes past without at least a couple of narrow gauge books being published. Recently there have been excellent books on the Fairlies of the Ffestiniog Railway and the locomotives of the Talyllyn and Corris railways. While it may seem that these are very specialist areas, the story of these locomotives is very much tied into the history of the railways and their operation. John Ransom's book *Narrow Gauge Steam* is a readable background to the history of steam locomotives on below standard gauge, and there are a number of other excellent books which concentrate on particular types of locomotive or their numerous builders. These range from a magisterial tome on Bagnalls of Stafford to this author's slim volume on the surviving steam locomotives of Fletcher Jennings & Company of Whitehaven.

More regular reading can be had from the printed *Narrow Gauge News*, published by and for members of the Narrow Gauge Railway Society – who also print the more in depth journal *The Narrow Gauge*. On wider circulation is the nationally available *Narrow Gauge World,* which looks at historic, preservation and modern aspects as well as modelling and international subjects. In the virtual world, the Narrow Gauge Net website is a vibrant and up to date e-journal which presents news and features on a regular basis, as well as promoting a variety of narrow gauge books from its publisher: https://www.mainlineandmaritime.co.uk/pages/welcome-to-narrow-gauge-net. Given the plethora of material out there, it is astounding that very little duplication occurs, especially when one considers that the mainstream media of *Railway Magazine* and *Steam Railway* magazine also carry monthly news sections!

The narrow gauge locomotive has come out from the shadows and into the spotlight. A key player in the industrial and transport history of the United Kingdom, it continues to be a major part of the tourist sector through the heritage industry across the country. As the railways declined after the Second Word War, who could have thought that over half a century later new locomotives were being built for new lines?

Left: Books on narrow gauge are plenty and varied, and have been published for over seventy years. From classic titles to esoteric byways, they have been written about. Here's a small section of narrow gauge books in the library of the National Railway Museum.

Below: I make no apology for ending the book with a photo of my favourite engine, Talyllyn Railway – former Corris Railway – No. 3 *Sir Haydn* at my favourite location, Rhydyronen, where our family used to have a static caravan and I stayed many times during my volunteer career, and where our young children were introduced to narrow gauge railways. This April 2010 photo coincided with the daffodils being out and the picture sums up to me the very special charm of the narrow gauge.